INVENTIONS AND DISCOVERY

CHARLES DARWIN
AND THE THEORY OF EVOLUTION

Heather Adamson

illustrated by Gordon Purcell
and Al Milgrom

www.raintreepublishers.co.uk
Visit our website to find out
more information about
Raintree books.

To order:
☎ Phone 0845 6044371
🖨 Fax +44 (0) 1865 312263
✉ Email myorders@capstonepub.co.uk

Customers from outside the UK please telephone +44 1865 312262

Raintree is an imprint of Capstone Global Library Limited, a company incorporated in England
and Wales having its registered office at 7 Pilgrim Street, London, EC4V 6LB – Registered company
number: 6695582

"Raintree" is a registered trademark of Pearson Education Limited, under licence to Capstone Global
Library Limited

Design: Thomas Emery and Kim Brown
Colourist: Krista Ward
UK editor: Diyan Leake
Originated by Capstone Global Library Ltd
Printed in China by South China Printing Company Ltd

ISBN 978 1 406 21568 7 (hardback)
14 13 12 11 10
10 9 8 7 6 5 4 3 2 1

British Library Cataloguing in Publication Data
Adamson, Heather -- Charles Darwin and the theory of evolution
A full catalogue record for this book is available from the British Library.

Every effort has been made to contact copyright holders of material reproduced in this book. Any
omissions will be rectified in subsequent printings if notice is given to the publisher.

Disclaimer
All the Internet addresses (URLs) given in this book were valid at the time of going to press. However,
due to the dynamic nature of the Internet, some addresses may have changed, or sites may have
changed or ceased to exist since publication. While the author and publisher regret any inconvenience
this may cause readers, no responsibility for any such changes can be accepted by either the author or
the publisher.

Editor's note: Direct quotations from primary sources are indicated by a yellow background.

Direct quotations appear on the following pages:
Page 7, quote from a letter by Darwin, as published in *The Life and Letters of Charles Darwin*, edited
by Francis Darwin (New York: D. Appleton & Co., 1901).
Page 16, from a 17 September 1835 entry in Darwin's *Beagle* diary (http://www.aboutdarwin.com/
voyage/voyage08.html).

CONTENTS

In 1831, Darwin received a letter from Henslow. Captain Robert FitzRoy would soon set sail on a voyage around the world. He wanted a naturalist to join in this adventure.

August 24, 1831 Charles, you are qualified for collecting, observing and noting anything worthy.

I've been asked to travel the world as a scientist, Father. My studies will finally prove useful.

I will not allow it. Many foolish young men have died following such crazy ideas.

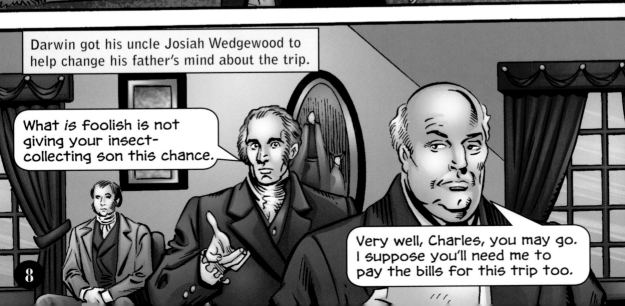

Darwin got his uncle Josiah Wedgewood to help change his father's mind about the trip.

What *is* foolish is not giving your insect-collecting son this chance.

Very well, Charles, you may go. I suppose you'll need me to pay the bills for this trip too.

At 27 metres (90 feet) long and 7 metres (24 feet) wide, HMS *Beagle* was a small ship. With about 70 people sharing the ship's cramped space, Darwin's life on the ship would be very different from his life in England.

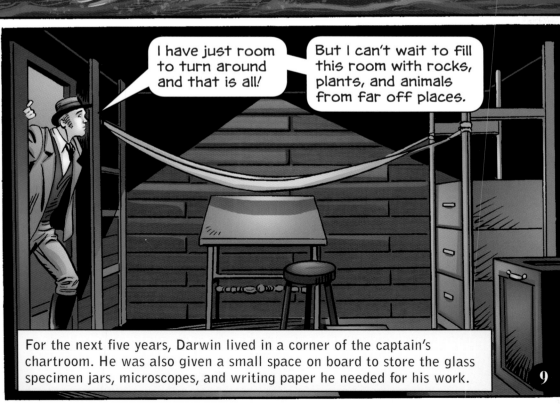

I have just room to turn around and that is all!

But I can't wait to fill this room with rocks, plants, and animals from far off places.

For the next five years, Darwin lived in a corner of the captain's chartroom. He was also given a small space on board to store the glass specimen jars, microscopes, and writing paper he needed for his work.

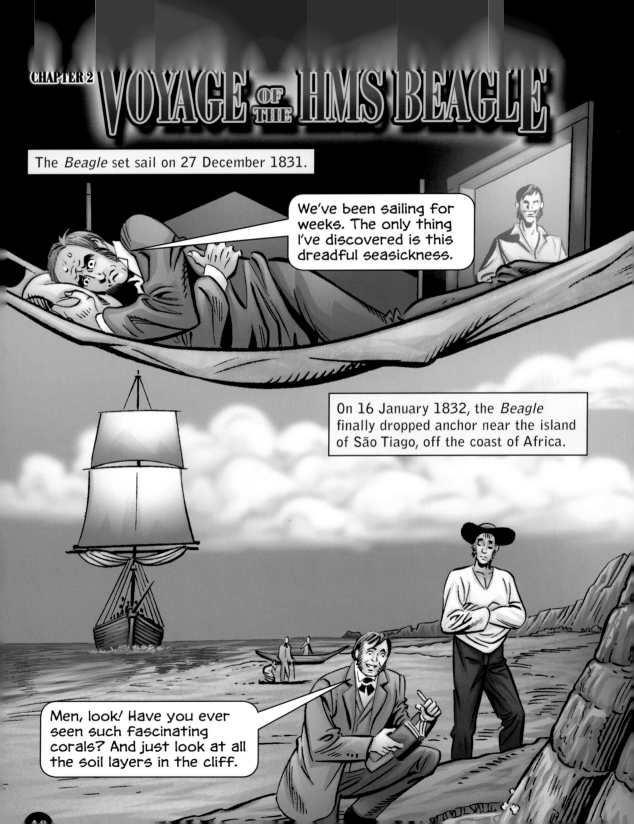

The *Beagle* continued its global trek. After crossing the equator, the ship landed in Brazil.

Humans seem like a tiny part of the living world. One species among countless others.

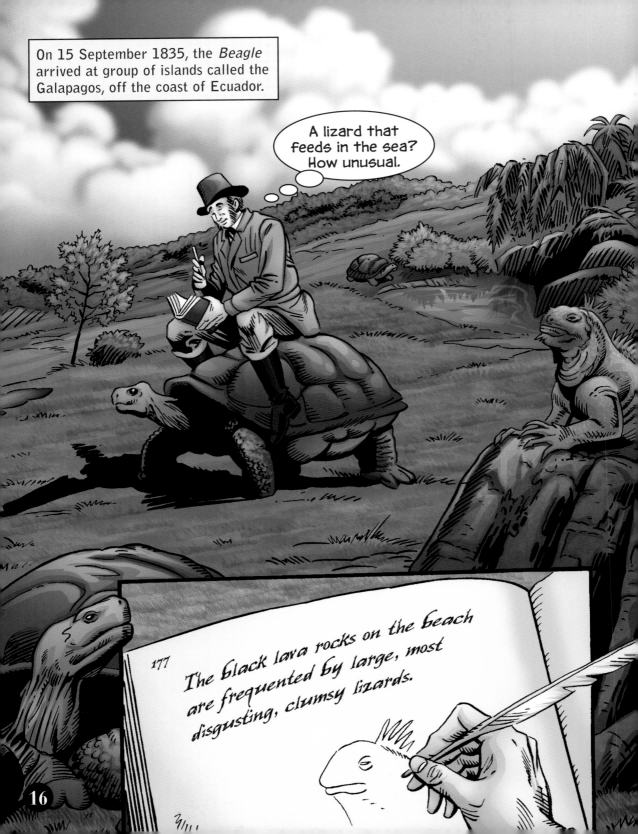

Darwin spent about a month studying the Galapagos before the *Beagle* continued its journey. On 2 October 1836, the *Beagle* arrived back in England.

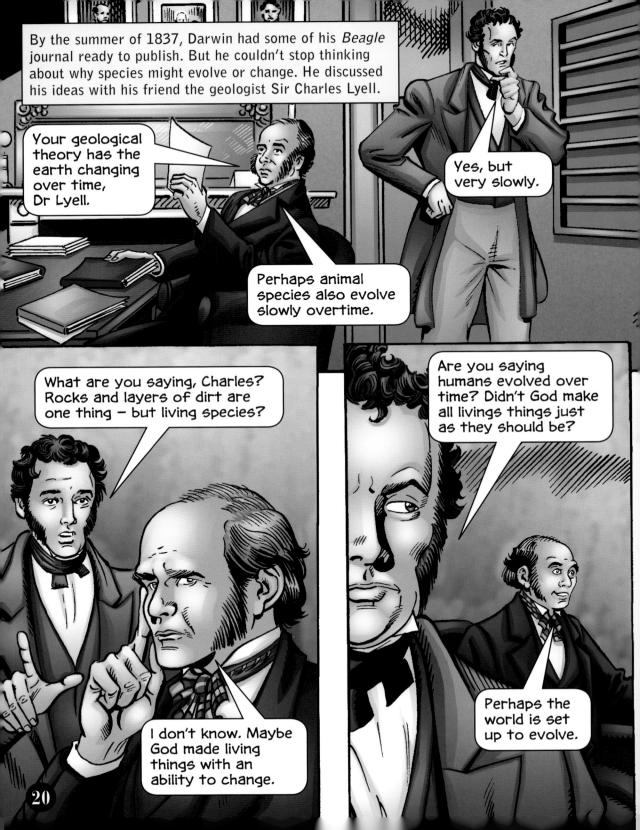

By 1854, Darwin was able to work on his ideas about how species evolve. Darwin studied cross-breeding in pigeons.

The striped birds and red birds will mate. Then we'll see what their chicks look like.

Perhaps nature works to get the best qualities in one species.

In the spring of 1856, Lyell visited Darwin.

I believe I know why species evolve.

They must compete to survive.

Animals and plants compete?

Yes, like two companies with the same product. The smarter one will be successful.

I don't know if I believe your theory, but I think it's time to share it.

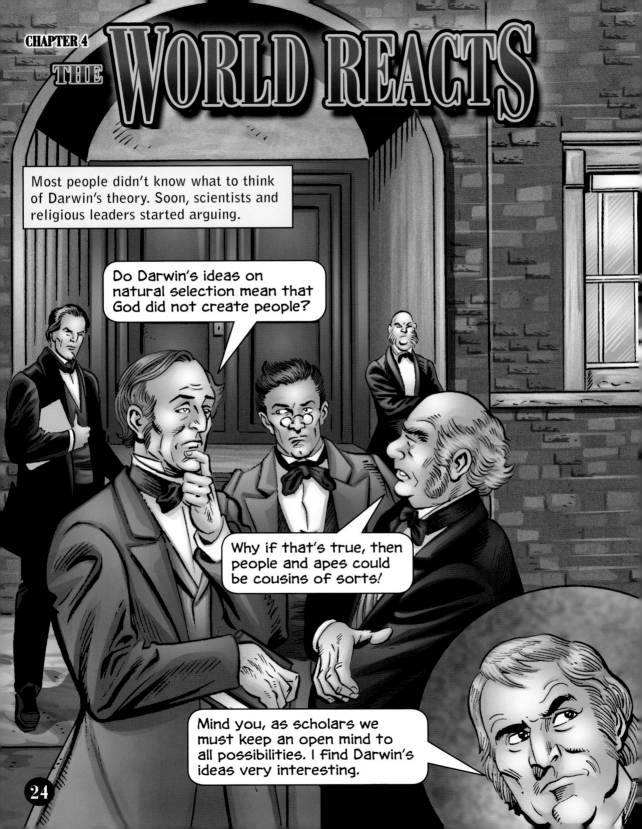

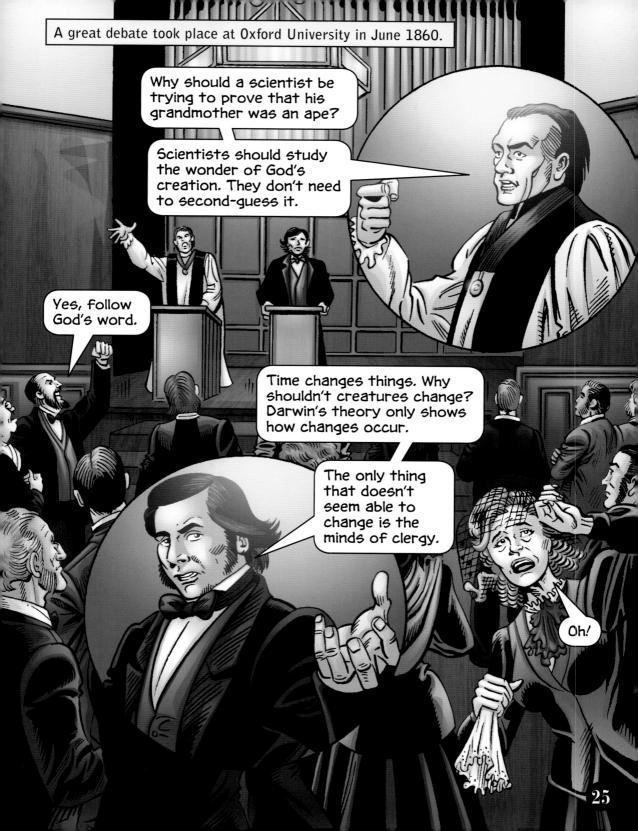

MORE ABOUT DARWIN
AND EVOLUTION

 Charles Darwin was born on 12 February 1809, in the town of Shrewsbury in Shropshire. Darwin struggled with illness for years after his *Beagle* voyage. He died on 19 April 1882, at his home in Kent.

 Ideas of evolution have been around for centuries. Even early Greek myths had ideas about species changing. Darwin's theory of natural selection was different because it addressed how and why species evolved.

 Darwin started "Notebook B" in July 1837. By November 1838, Darwin's ideas and questions had expanded into notebooks "C", "D", "E", "M", and "N".

 A 1925 court case, *Scopes versus State,* sparked a debate about Darwin and the teaching of evolution. The case became known as the Scopes Monkey Trial. Reporters from around the world covered the case.

 Darwin was known as an unusual father. Most wealthy Englishmen did not spend much time with their children. Instead, they paid workers to care for them. But Darwin played with his children. He took them for walks and let them help in his lab. He was their favourite playmate.

Darwin first grew his famous beard in 1866. Some say he grew it so people wouldn't recognize him in public.

 Darwin was often sick in bed and he passed the time writing letters. More than 15,000 letters to and from Darwin have been collected by Cambridge University.

 While travelling in South America, Darwin was often bitten by assassin bugs. These blood-sucking beetles can carry Chagas' disease. Darwin describes being attacked by the bugs: "It is most disgusting to feel soft wingless insects, about an inch long, crawling over one's body. Before sucking they are quite thin, but afterward they become round and bloated with blood, and in this state are easily crushed."

 In honour of his curiosity and research, Darwin has had many things named after him, including the Galapagos finches, an ostrich-like bird called a rhea, a mountain, and even a European space mission.

GLOSSARY

adapt change to fit into a different or new environment

cross-breed cross two varieties or breeds of the same species by mating

DNA material in cells that gives people, plants, and animals their individual characteristics

evolve develop over a long time with gradual changes

petrified wood wood that has been changed into a stony substance by water and minerals

species group of plants or animals that share common characteristics

specimen sample or example used to stand for a whole group

INTERNET SITES

http://www.nhm.ac.uk
Click on the "Nature online" tab, then on "The science of natural history" menu to get "Natural history biographies" for more information and a short video on Charles Darwin and his work.

http://www.darwin200.org/
Go to this website for information on a national programme of events honouring Charles Darwin's scientific ideas and their impact. More information can be found in the "About Charles Darwin" and "Darwin's Britain" menus.

MORE BOOKS TO READ

Charles Darwin (Levelled Biographies: Great Naturalists series), Heidi Moore (Heinemann Library, 2008)

Charles Darwin, David C. King (Dorling Kindersley, 2006)

The Evolution Revolution, Robert Winston (Dorling Kindersley, 2009)

How Does a Bone Become a Fossil?, Melissa Stewart (Raintree, 2010)

On the Origin of Species: The Illustrated Edition, Charles Darwin (Sterling, 2008)

One Beetle Too Many: The Extraordinary Adventures of Charles Darwin, Kathy Lasky and Matthew Trueman (Candlewick, 2009)

FIND OUT MORE

Watch *Creation* (2009), a film starring Paul Bettany and Jennifer Connelly, set during the time that Darwin was writing *On the Origin of Species*.

Visit the home where Charles Darwin lived for 40 years and wrote *On the Origin of Species*:
Down House, Luxted Road
Downe, Kent BR6 7JT
http://www.english-heritage.org.uk/server/show/nav.14922

See scientists at work, specimens, displays, the Attenborough Studio, and more at the Darwin Centre in the Cocoon Building at the Natural History Museum.
Natural History Museum
Cromwell Road, London SW7 5BD
Telephone: 0207 942 5000
http://www.nhm.ac.uk/visit-us/darwin-centre-visitors/getting-to-darwin-centre/index.html

INDEX